BASIC/NOT BORING LANGUAGE SKILLS

GRAMMAR & USAGE

Grades 4-5

Inventive Exercises to Sharpen
Skills and Raise Achievement

Series Concept & Development
by Imogene Forte & Marjorie Frank

Exercises by Diana Standing

Illustrations by Gayle Harvey

Incentive Publications, Inc.
Nashville, Tennessee

About the cover:
Bound resist, or tie dye, is the most ancient known method of fabric surface design. The brilliance of the basic tie dye design on this cover reflects the possibilities that emerge from the mastery of basic skills.

Cover art by Mary Patricia Deprez, dba Tye Dye Mary®
Cover design by Marta Drayton, Joe Shibley, and W. Paul Nance
Edited by Anna Quinn

ISBN 0-86530-400-9

2   3   4   5   6   7   8   9   10   08   07   06   05

PRINTED IN THE UNITED STATES OF AMERICA
www.incentivepublications.com

TABLE OF CONTENTS

CELEBRATE BASIC LANGUAGE SKILLS

Basic does not mean boring! There certainly is nothing dull about . . .

   . . . sharing scary ghost stories around a campfire

   . . . getting lost in the woods or escaping a rock slide

   . . . joining a wonderful food fight in
      the camp mess hall

   . . . wondering if Bigfoot is really out there
      just beyond your tent site

   . . . wondering if that light in the sky really is a UFO

   . . . taking part in wild river rafting and other exciting camp adventures

   . . . trying to identify the unrecognizable food cooked in the camp kitchen

   . . . finding out the truth about what really happened on the midnight hike

These are just some of the adventures students can explore as they celebrate basic language skills. The idea of celebrating the basics is just what it sounds like—enjoying and improving the skills of using the English language. Each page invites learners to try a high-interest, appealing exercise that will sharpen one specific grammar or usage skill. This is no ordinary fill-in-the-blanks way to learn! These exercises are fun and surprising. Students will do the useful work of practicing language skills while they enjoy looking in on the many wacky adventures of the campers and staff at Camp Lookout!

The pages in this book can be used in many ways:

- to sharpen or review a grammar or usage skill with one student
- to reinforce the skill with a small or large group
- by students working on their own
- by students working under the direction of a parent or teacher

Each page may be used to introduce a new skill, reinforce a skill, or assess a student's ability to perform a skill. There's more than just the great student activity pages. You will also find an appendix of resources for students and teachers—including a ready-to-use test for assessing grammar and usage skills.

The pages are written with the assumption that an adult will be available to assist the student with their learning and practice. Also, students will need to have resources available for completing some of the grammar and usage activities.

As your students take on the challenges of these adventures with language, they will grow! And as you watch them check off the basic language skills they've strengthened, you can celebrate with them!

The Skills Test

Use the skills test beginning on page 56 as a pretest and/or a post-test. This will help you check the students' mastery of grammar and usage skills and will prepare them for success on achievement tests.

SKILLS CHECKLIST FOR
GRAMMAR & USAGE, Grades 4-5

✔	SKILL	PAGE(S)
	Identify and write declarative, interrogative, imperative, and exclamatory sentences	10
	Find simple subjects and simple predicates	11
	Identify and write simple and compound sentences	12
	Identify and correct sentence fragments and run-on sentences	13
	Distinguish among parts of speech	14–32, 34–36
	Identify and use common and proper nouns	15–19
	Identify and use singular and plural nouns	16–19
	Identify, form, and use singular possessive nouns	18
	Identify, form, and use plural possessive nouns	19
	Identify and use subject and object pronouns	20, 21
	Identify and use verb tenses: past, present, and future	22–25
	Identify and use irregular verbs	25
	Identify and use action verbs	26
	Identify and use helping verbs	27
	Identify and use adjectives	28, 30, 31
	Identify and use adverbs	29, 32
	Identify and use comparative and superlative adjectives	30, 31
	Identify and use comparative and superlative adverbs	32
	Use negatives correctly; correct double negatives	33
	Identify and use prepositions and prepositional phrases	34, 35
	Identify and use direct objects	36
	Identify and distinguish among homophones	37–39
	Identify and form contractions	40
	Make corrections in improper capitalization	41–43, 45, 47, 50–51
	Use proper capitalization in a variety of situations	41–43, 46, 47, 50–52
	Use proper capitalization for sentences, proper nouns, and adjectives	41–43, 46, 47, 50–51
	Properly use a variety of punctuation marks	44–46, 50–52
	Make corrections in improper punctuation	44–46, 50–52
	Correct spelling in a variety of situations	48–51
	Use quotation marks properly in dialogue	52

GRAMMAR & USAGE

Skills Exercises

WHERE IS CAMP LOOKOUT?

All over the country, people are talking about wild and wacky Camp Lookout. Read the sentences below. Punctuate each sentence correctly, and then label it according to the box below. Use the clues in the sentences to help you unscramble the name of the state in which the camp is located.

> Kinds of sentences:
> **Interrogative sentences** (I) ask a question and end with a question mark.
> **Exclamatory sentences** (E) express strong feelings and end with an exclamation point.
> **Imperative sentences** (IM) give an order and end with a period.
> **Declarative sentences** tell (D) something and end with a period.

_____ 1. How do we get to Camp Lookout

_____ 2. Find the atlas

_____ 3. There have been Bigfoot sightings in that region of the United States

_____ 4. Many mountains, rivers, and lakes are found there

_____ 5. Don't get too close to the waterfalls when you're rafting

_____ 6. Get your fishing pole ready

_____ 7. Your tent is falling down

_____ 8. Which ghost story was too scary

_____ 9. Is that plant poison oak

_____ 10. Stay away from the bears

_____ 11. The camp is in a state that borders the Pacific Ocean

_____ 12. Oh, no, there's a skunk in our tent

_____ 13. You'll never forget Camp Lookout

The scrambled name of the state is NHGONWISAT.

Unscrambled, it is _____.

Now write your own example of each kind of sentence.

Interrogative _____

Exclamatory _____

Imperative _____

Declarative _____

Name

STEP BY STEP

Campers must be careful when climbing the rickety ladder to the tree house at Camp Lookout. If you can catch the subject and predicate in the sentence for each rung of the ladder, they will get to the top before it collapses. Start with Rung #10. Circle the simple subject for each sentence. Underline the simple predicate for each sentence.

> The **subject** tells who or what is doing something.
> The **predicate** tells what the subject is doing.
> *Example: Sometimes the mother bear growls at her cubs.*
> The **simple subject** is **bear**.
> The **simple predicate** is **growls**.

10. The tree house is reached at last!

9. Sometimes a coyote howls.

8. Sometimes an owl hoots.

7. Squirrels jump from limb to limb.

6. A swinging rope hangs from one of the branches.

5. Birds have built a nest in the tree.

4. Moss is growing on the roof.

3. Some of the boards are falling off.

2. The tree house looks old.

1. The ladder shakes with each step.

Name

CAMPER CARL'S COMPOUND PROBLEM

> A **simple sentence** is a group of words that expresses a complete thought.
>
> A **compound sentence** combines two, related simple sentences with the conjunctions *and, or,* or *but.*
>
> *Examples:*
>   *Simple sentence:* Four campers went horseback riding.
>   *Compound sentence:* Four campers went horseback riding, and two of them were riding bareback.

Counselor I. M. Wacky is at it again! He has asked Carl to solve a strange problem. Please help Carl with this problem.

1. Read each sentence below carefully. Write **S** for simple or **C** for compound in the blank before each sentence.
2. Try to find a way for Carl to get to the other side of the lake with the instructions Counselor Wacky gave him.

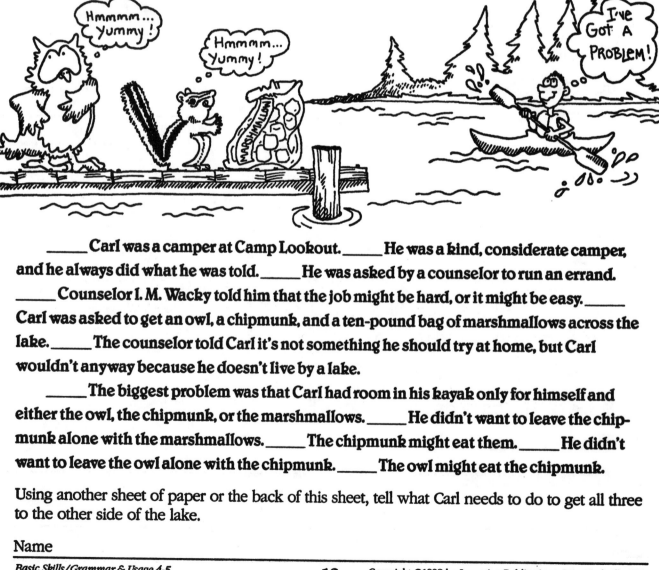

_____ Carl was a camper at Camp Lookout. _____ He was a kind, considerate camper, and he always did what he was told. _____ He was asked by a counselor to run an errand.

_____ Counselor I. M. Wacky told him that the job might be hard, or it might be easy. _____ Carl was asked to get an owl, a chipmunk, and a ten-pound bag of marshmallows across the lake. _____ The counselor told Carl it's not something he should try at home, but Carl wouldn't anyway because he doesn't live by a lake.

_____ The biggest problem was that Carl had room in his kayak only for himself and either the owl, the chipmunk, or the marshmallows. _____ He didn't want to leave the chipmunk alone with the marshmallows. _____ The chipmunk might eat them. _____ He didn't want to leave the owl alone with the chipmunk. _____ The owl might eat the chipmunk.

Using another sheet of paper or the back of this sheet, tell what Carl needs to do to get all three to the other side of the lake.

Name _____

RUNNING OUT OF CONTROL

Boulders are running out of control! Rewrite the run-on sentences and fragments correctly, before the boulders go crashing into Camp Lookout!

1. The boulders rolled slowly at first they gathered speed soon after.

2. Steep mountain.

3. Tremendous force.

4. Crashing noises.

5. The boulders crushed plants animals scampered away quickly.

6. The forest service ranger.

7. They gained speed over and over they rolled.

8. When the oak tree fell.

9. Was spinning and settling.

10. The boulders are approaching Camp Lookout will they stop in time

LOOKOUT, LOOKOUT!

CAMP LOOKOUT

A **run-on sentence** contains two or more sentences that have not been separated by the proper punctuation or connecting words.

A **fragment** is part of a sentence that does not express a complete thought.

1. _____

_____

2. _____

_____

3. _____

_____

4. _____

_____

5. _____

_____

6. _____

_____

7. _____

8. _____

9. _____

10. _____

Name _____

SMOOTH SAILING

Follow the directions to color the picture of campers sailing on Agate Lake at Camp Lookout. First, label the nouns (N), adjectives (ADJ), verbs (V), and adverbs (ADV) in the sentences below. Then find the words from each sentence in the picture. If the word is a noun, color it yellow. If the word is a verb, color it green. If the word is an adjective, color it red. If the word is an adverb, color it brown.

> A **noun** is a person, place, or thing.
> A **verb** tells what the noun does.
> An **adjective** describes the noun.
> An **adverb** describes the verb.
> *Example: The big raccoon ate slowly.*
> **Big** *is an adjective.*
> **Raccoon** *is a noun.*
> **Ate** *is a verb.*
> **Slowly** *is an adverb.*

1. The wooden boat sailed smoothly.
2. The north wind blew hard.
3. A colorful sail flapped gracefully.
4. Often a brown squirrel chews acorns on the boat dock.
5. The deer were walking slowly along the shore.
6. Sometimes a curious raccoon rides on one of the sailboats.
7. The goofy camper fell awkwardly into the water.
8. Two campers swam quickly to rescue their friend.

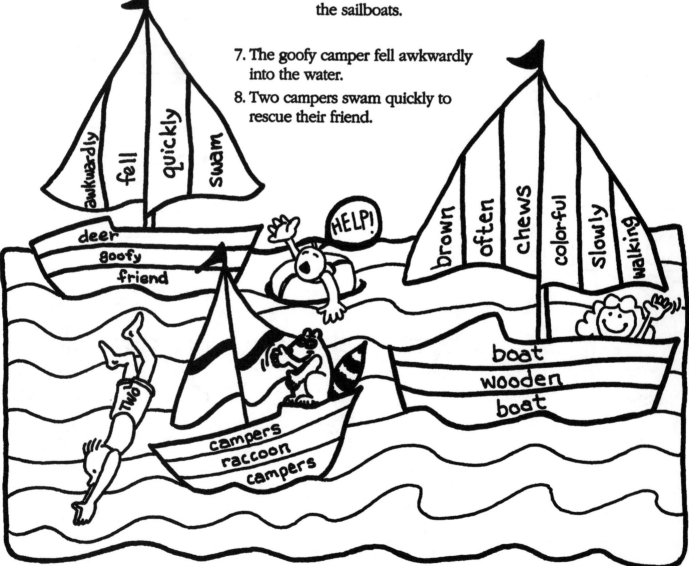

KEY CREATURES

Lisa has found herself in an uncomfortable situation. You'll soon figure out why. Try to find the route she is taking as she searches for the key to the outhouse door. Follow the directions carefully. Do one sentence at a time.

> **Common nouns** refer to persons, places, or things in general.
> *Example: lake*
> **Proper nouns** refer to a specific person, place, or thing.
> *Example: Agate Lake*

1. **Circle all the nouns. Put a C above the common nouns and a P above the proper nouns.**

2. **Find a picture of one of the nouns in the maze below.**

3. **Use the picture clues from each sentence to trace her route.**

    1. Lisa couldn't find the key to the outhouse.

    2. Last Friday, Billy had taken the key and given it to a raccoon.

    3. As Lisa walked along the trail, a snake crossed her path.

    4. Next a coyote howled.

    5. She wondered if the chipmunk she saw near a stump had the key.

    6. An old owl called, "Who, who," and she wondered who took the key.

    7. A bear was picking berries in a patch.

    8. A rabbit hopped away.

    9. She wandered close to the shore of Blue River and saw a beaver gnawing on a tree.

    10. A skunk surprised Lisa and almost made her lose her way.

    11. Huge animal tracks reminded her of the ones she'd seen last August.

    12. The tracks led to the outhouse door!

Name _____

THE GREENHORNS CAMP OUT

MUST BE CITY BOYS...

Justin and Isaac decided to go camping on their own, away from Camp Lookout. It was their first camping experience. Read to see how these greenhorns managed. (Find out what greenhorn means!)

In the sentences below, make the noun in parentheses plural.

Singular is one.

Plural is more than one.

To form plurals:

> **Add s** to most singular nouns.
>
> **Add es** to nouns ending in **x, s, ch,** or **sh.**
>
> **Add s** to nouns ending in a **vowel and y.**
>
> When the letter before an ending **y** is a consonant, change the **y** to **i** and add **es.**

1. Justin and Isaac decided to take their tent to an area near several _____. (marsh)

2. They were from big _____ and hadn't had any camping experience. (city)

3. They brought _____ to help them with directions. (compass)

4. They talked about school and some of their favorite _____ . (holiday)

5. They sang some of their favorite camp _____ . (song)

6. Two _____ could be seen in the distance. (fox)

7. Deer watched from the _____ as they tried to set up their tent. (bush)

8. The _____ kept falling down after each one was hammered in. (pole)

9. There were _____ of poison oak nearby. (bunch)

10. After building a campfire, Justin cut one of the _____ from a poison oak bush without realizing what it was. (branch)

11. He removed the leaves and took out a package of _____ . (marshmallow)

12. The _____ moaned that evening when, as they curled up in their sleeping _____ , the tent collapsed again. (camper, bag)

Name _____

A GRAND MESS IN THE MESS HALL

Stay clear of the camp dining area, the mess hall. There are some strange things going on! The sentences tell about them. As you read them, write the plural form of the singular noun in the blank provided.

> To make these singular nouns **plural:**
> If it ends in **f** or **fe,** change the **f** to **v** and add **es** or **s.**
> If it ends with a **vowel and o,** add **s.**
> If it ends with a **consonant and o,** add **es** to some and **s** to others.
> Some plural nouns have **different spellings** (foot—feet; child—children).
> Some nouns are the **same** in singular and plural forms (sheep; deer).

1. No one could understand how _____ ended up in the mess hall. (sheep)

2. Food began flying when several _____ ran across the floor. (mouse)

3. _____ of the campers' voices rang through the hall. (echo)

4. Three _____ were hit in the face with pizza. (child)

5. Carl had cheese dripping from his chin, while Lisa was hit with mashed _____. (potato)

6. Manuel lost two _____ trying to eat a slice of bread. (tooth)

7. The _____ of bread were so hard, the _____ could barely cut through them. (loaf, knife)

8. Several campers didn't like the _____ that were served. (trout)

9. One camper threw his trout across the room, and it landed on a tray of sliced _____. (tomato)

10. Someone turned up the volume on all the _____ so no one could hear anything except squealing and music. (radio)

11. Then some of the campers began stomping their _____. (foot)

12. The Camp Lookout counselors' _____ would never be the same. (life)

13. The place looked as if it had entertained a stampeding herd of _____. (moose)

Name

PICTURE THE OWNER

Lots of things get lost at Camp Lookout. Campers and counselors are always trying to find out who owns what! You can show ownership (possession) by changing words. Add **'s** to the words in Column A so they will show possession. Then match the words in Column A with the words in Column B, and write them above or below each picture. The first one is done for you.

> To make a **singular noun** show **ownership** add **'s**.

A		**B**	
1. tent	5. rabbit	ears	footprints
2. skunk	6. counselor	compass	door
3. camper	7. Bigfoot	T-shirt	poles
4. tree house	8. fox	teeth	babies

6. _____

5. _____

3. _____

7. _____

4. _____

2. _____

1. tent's poles

8. _____

Now write three sentences using the singular possessive forms of any of the nouns above.

1. _____

2. _____

3. _____

Name _____

18

LOST & FOUND

More stuff is missing at Camp Lookout! There are some strange things in the Lost & Found. Use the rule about plural possessives to add either **'s** or an **'** by itself to the words in Column A so they will show possession. Then match the words in Column A with the words in Column B, and write them above or below each picture. The first one is done for you.

> To make a **plural noun** show **ownership** add **'s**.
> If the word already ends in **s**, add an **'** only.

A		**B**	
1. flowers	5. campers	tails	caps
2. children	6. deer	treasure map	aprons
3. cooks	7. boats	petals	sails
4. mice	8. counselors	sleeping bags	food

5. _____

8. _____

3. _____

2. _____

7. _____

4. _____

6. _____

flowers' petals

Write three sentences using the plural possessive forms of any of the nouns above.

1. _____

2. _____

3. _____

Name _____

PACK RATS

Maria and Heidi are getting ready for their two-week visit to Camp Lookout. They're having a hard time fitting everything into the trunk! Read the sentences that tell about their packing. Look for **subject pronouns.** Circle any that you find. Notice that not every sentence has one!

A **pronoun** is used to replace a noun. **Subject pronouns** replace the subject.

*Examples: **I, we, they, he, she, it,** and* **you.**

*She lost the key. (**She** is the subject pronoun.)*

---

1. The two girls studied the map of Camp Lookout.

2. "It looks so exciting!"

3. Maria and Heidi were packing for their trip.

4. They checked each other's list.

5. Maria had forgotten to include a flashlight.

6. She also forgot to pack a camera.

7. Heidi had packed too much.

8. She couldn't close her suitcase.

9. "I could take less."

10. Maria couldn't decide where to put her fishing gear.

11. The last piece of luggage would not fit in the trunk of Maria's father's car.

12. "You have too much stuff."

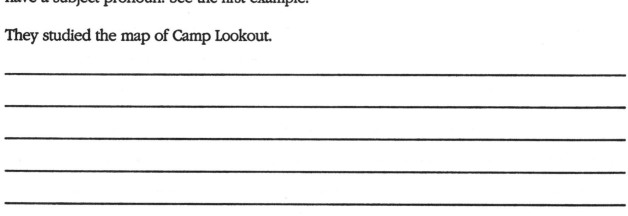

Rewrite the sentences that did not have subject pronouns. Make sure your new sentences each have a subject pronoun. See the first example.

They studied the map of Camp Lookout.

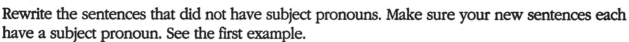

_____

_____

_____

_____

Name

GETTING THERE

The pack rats have finished packing. Now Maria and Heidi are finally on their way to Camp Lookout! Circle the object pronouns in the sentences below, and learn about their ride to camp.

A **pronoun** is used to replace a noun.

Object pronouns replace nouns used after action verbs.

*Examples: **them, us, it, her, him, me,** and **you**.*

*Campers bring them to their cabins. (**Them** is the object pronoun.)*

1. In the car, Maria's father told us about his childhood.

2. Heidi asked him how long he lived in Mexico.

3. He told her twenty years.

4. At noon her father showed them his favorite restaurant.

5. The waitress gave us seats with a view of the pond.

6. Although the food was good, Heidi couldn't eat it all.

7. Maria's father showed us many different kinds of wildlife along the way.

8. He described them in detail.

9. Maria helped me roll down the window to get a better look at the animals.

10. We wanted them to come with us to camp.

11. We didn't ask him to stop.

12. At last we arrived. Maria's father drove us straight to the Camp Lookout Office.

Use some of the object pronouns listed above to create your own sentences. Remember that the object pronoun follows an action verb. It receives the action of the verb.

1. _____

_____

_____

2. _____

_____

_____

Name _____

AGATE LAKE

Agate Lake is a bustling center of
activities at Camp Lookout. Read
about what is going on now at
the lake. Fill in the blank in each
sentence with the present tense
form of the verb. The first one is
done for you.

1. The sun ____*shines*____ brightly over Agate Lake. (shine)

2. Campers _____ on the lake. (sail)

3. Others _____ their boats. (row)

4. Some campers _____ in the lake. (fish)

5. Animals _____ from the lake. (drink)

6. A large fish _____ water near a boat when it jumps. (splash)

7. A deer _____ from the nearby bushes. (watch)

8. Carl and Manuel _____ a campfire. (build)

9. They _____ hot dogs and marshmallows. (roast)

10. A marshmallow _____ off the stick into the fire. (fall)

11. Ann _____ rocks on the water. (skip)

12. Maria and Lisa _____ near the boat dock. (swim)

> Besides
> showing
> action,
> **verbs** also
> tell when
> the action
> happened.
> A **present
> tense verb**
> tells what is
> happening
> right now.

Write a short story telling about something else that might happen at Lake Agate. Use present
tense verbs in the sentences to tell what is happening **now.**

_____

_____

_____

_____

_____

_____

_____

Name

BLUE RIVER

Blue River is a popular place for the campers at Camp Lookout. Find out why in the following sentences. Read the sentences, and fill in each blank with the **past tense form of the verb.** The first one is done for you.

> A **past tense verb** tells what has already happened.
> Regular past tense verbs are formed by adding either **ed** or **d.**

1. Carl __*watched*__ many rafters paddle by him on the Blue River. (watch)
2. The rafters were _____ with water when they went through the rapids. (spray)
3. Justin _____ in a still, deep pool of water. (fish)
4. A beaver _____ on a tree. (chew)
5. An eagle _____ overhead. (hover)
6. Maria and Lisa _____ stories while they were rafting. (share)
7. They _____ about their classes at school. (talk)
8. Maria _____ favorite books she had read. (suggest)
9. Lisa _____ ideas for tricks to play on cabin counselors. (propose)
10. An otter _____ close to their raft. (move)
11. It _____ on its back. (float)
12. They _____ watching the otter. (enjoy)

Write a story telling about something else that might have happened on Blue River. Use **regular past tense verbs** in the sentences to tell what **already happened.**

_____

_____

_____

_____

_____

_____

Name _____

BEAR CREEK

Bear Creek is well named. Many bears have been spotted in the area. Campers are warned to be careful. Find out what will be happening soon at Bear Creek by filling in the blanks with the future tense of the verbs. The first one is done for you.

> A **future tense** verb tells what is going to happen.
>
> To form the future tense, add the helping verbs **will** or **shall** to the main verb.
>
> *Example: Sam **will fall** in the creek today.*

1. Isaac and his cabin roommates ___*will go*___ to Bear Creek. (go)

2. They _____ the creek environment. (study)

3. Manuel _____ nets for scooping up larvae and eggs. (bring)

4. Billy _____ to find a frog for the frog jumping contest. (try)

5. Carl _____ his binoculars for bird watching. (take)

6. Some of the birds _____ nesting. (be)

7. They _____ food during the day. (find)

8. The baby birds _____ only at night. (fly)

9. The counselor _____ for bear tracks. (look)

10. The bear _____ berries near the creek. (eat)

11. They _____ for their cubs who are searching for berries also. (care)

12. We _____ the cubs and their mothers do not come too close. (hope)

Write a short story telling about something that might happen at Bear Creek in the future. Use future tense verbs in the sentences to tell what **will happen.**

_____

_____

_____

_____

Name _____

IRREGULAR BEINGS

There are some strange, out-of-this-world happenings at Camp Lookout. Read the sentences and fill in the blanks with the correct form of the irregular verbs to discover what is happening. The first one is done for you.

> **Regular past tense verbs** are formed by adding **ed** or **d**.
>
> **Irregular past tense verbs** show what has happened in the past by using a special form.
>
> *Example: Present tense—go, write.*
> *Past tense—went, wrote.*

1. Carl __*thought*__ the sky had suddenly become an eerie pink color. (think)

2. As Manuel looked straight ahead he _____ something land in a meadow. (see)

3. Carl and Manuel _____ behind some trees and peeked around to see an unusual spacecraft in the distance. (hide)

4. The light around the spacecraft _____ brighter. (grow)

5. A tiny being, four inches tall, _____ out. Its antennas seemed to be sending signals. (come)

6. It was green and _____ something that looked like polka-dotted pajamas. (wear)

7. It picked and _____ some grass in the meadow. (eat)

8. It _____ very close to where Carl and Manuel were hiding. (go)

9. It _____ when it saw them. (run)

10. Almost as quickly as it had appeared, the spacecraft _____ out of sight. (fly)

11. Manuel and Carl quickly headed for Camp Lookout where they _____ everyone their exciting news. (tell)

12. They also _____ home to tell their parents. (write)

Write a sentence or two about a strange happening. Use some irregular past tense verbs in your sentences.

_____

_____

_____

Name _____

GHOST STORY

There was lots of action last night in one of the girls' cabins. A full moon was the backdrop for the ghost story Heidi decided to tell her cabin mates. Circle the action verbs in the story.

> **Scream, leap, swallow,** and **gobbled** are **action verbs** because they show action.
> **Was, were,** and **am** are not action verbs. They are **passive.**

Heidi's story began . . .

It was midnight. The only sounds were the ticking clock and the blowing window shutters. Suddenly, from her bed, the old woman noticed a hand that appeared outside on the window ledge. The fingers scratched at the window. They wiggled up and down as if they were playing a piano. Then she heard a voice whisper, "Where are my creepy fingers?" The dog crawled under her bed. The old woman sat up. She tried to figure out where the voice was coming from. This time the voice was louder, "Where are my creepy fingers?"

The old woman noticed that the hand didn't seem attached to anything. She listened. The window creaked and opened. The hand moved inside. The old woman hid under the covers. The voice got louder, "Give me my creepy fingers." The woman hid deeper under the covers and pillows. She heard an even louder voice. "Give me my creepy fingers!"

At this point Heidi grabbed Lisa, who jumped out of bed screaming.

Write a few sentences telling what would have happened next in this story.
Use lots of action verbs.

Name _____

SURVIVAL TRAINING

Carl is lost in the woods. Find the helping verb and the item in each sentence that will help Carl survive and get back to Camp Lookout. Circle each helping verb. When you find the item in the sentence, look for it in the maze. Be sure to find the items step by step, in order. This will show the correct path for Carl to follow to get back.

> **Helping verbs** are sometimes used with main action verbs.
> **Common helping verbs:** has, had, have, should, shall, will, were, are, was, am, is.

1. He is wearing the pants without a whistle in the pocket.
2. The matches were sitting on the mess hall table.
3. He will try to understand how to use the compass.
4. He is going to find materials to make a shelter.
5. Carl has seen water near the alien sighting.
6. He had taken the knife to the arts and crafts center for soap carving.
7. He has left a blanket under the bed.
8. I am afraid the flashlight was left near the boat dock.
9. He remembers he should gather wood to build a fire.
10. Then he will look for berries.
11. Near the food, he should see the entrance to the camp.
12. His friends are hoping he will find his way back to camp.

Name

A SCRAMBLED MENU

Campers are smelling some unusual odors, which seem to be coming from the mess hall. Check the menu below to see what's cooking. Underline the adjectives in the sentences below. The first sentence is completed for you.

> An **adjective** is a word that describes a noun.
>
> *Example: The unusual odors bothered us.*
>
> **Unusual** *is an adjective describing the noun.*

BREAKFAST MENU
☆ SCRAMBLED EMU EGGS WITH PURPLE HAM!
☆ FRENCH TOAST TOPPED WITH DANDELION SYRUP!
HAVE A GREAT DAY!

LUNCH MENU
☆ PEANUT BUTTER AND PAPAYA SANDWICH!
☆ GRILLED CHEESE WITH SARDINE SANDWICH!
EAT HEARTY!

DINNER MENU
☆ FROG LEGS SAUTÉD IN A LEMON SAUCE!
☆ PIZZA TOPPED WITH GOAT CHEESE, TROUT, AND SPINACH!
HAPPY DINING!

1. The slimy, gooey eggs tasted terrible.

2. The crunchy, purple ham broke a tooth.

3. Isaac complained that old, moldy bread was used to make the sandwiches.

4. One of the clumsy cooks dropped a plate of French toast topped with dandelion syrup.

5. The muddy, thick, cold hot chocolate got stuck in Maria's throat.

6. One of the counselors had a tiny, tasty frog leg sticking out of his mouth.

7. Heidi couldn't eat the strange, sticky pizza.

8. Hungry Carl didn't choose to eat the weird grilled cheese sandwich.

Justin used three of the adjectives from above to describe Camp Lookout's food. Unscramble the letters to see what they are.

atgersn _____   ilsym _____   lmdyo _____

Write your own ideas for a menu for the camp's mess hall. Use lots of tasty adjectives!

_____

_____

_____

Name

CAMPFIRE PROCEDURES

CAMPFIRE MEETING PROCEDURES

1. Immediately bring a flashlight and your songbook.
2. Walk slowly.
3. Wait patiently until it is time to find a seat.
4. When told, sit down carefully.
5. Open your songbook and hold it firmly.
6. Do not race through the song quickly.
7. Sing loudly or softly depending on the instructions of the song leader.
8. Watch the leader closely.
9. Do not begin the songs early.
10. Now sing the theme song for Camp Lookout cheerfully and clearly.

If you're going to be a camper at Camp Lookout, you need to learn the proper procedures to follow when gathering around the evening campfire. Read these rules, and circle all the adverbs.

An **adverb** is a word that describes a verb. Adverbs tell **how, when, where,** and **how often.**

Example: The camper walked cheerfully to the campfire.

Cheerfully *is the adverb that describes how she walked.*

CAMP LOOKOUT
We Love Camp Lookout
Oh yes we do......
There can't be anything
As weird as you......
When we're not here at camp
We're bluuue !
Oh, Camp Lookout we love you !

WET, WETTER, WETTEST

Campers will be testing their skills at the Camp Lookout Water Competition. Write the correct form of the adjective in these sentences about the competition. The first one is done for you.

> **Er** is added to most adjectives to compare two things.
>
> **Est** is added to most adjectives to compare more than two things.

1. Carl had the ___*tiniest*___ balloon in the water balloon toss. (tiny)
2. Manuel's balloon was _____ than his friend Nick's. (large)
3. Unfortunately, Isaac had the _____ balloon, which broke on Carl's head. (big)
4. Carl became the _____ camper at Camp Lookout. (wet)
5. Ann was the last one to arrive for the frog jumping contest. She was the _____ . (late)
6. She found her frog, which was the _____ , in a nearby swamp. (slimy)
7. Maria's frog was the _____ in the competition. (small)
8. After much debate, it was decided that her frog jumped the _____ . (farther)
9. Nick's frog was the _____ . (fat)
10. It surprised everyone when his frog jumped the _____ . (high)
11. The kayaking competition took the _____ time. (long)
12. Carl was _____ than Isaac. (fast)
13. Eventually Isaac and Manuel fell out of their kayaks, so they were the _____ . (slow)
14. Although Ann paddled the _____ of all the campers, Maria won the race. (fast)

At the end of these activities and other Water Competition events, there were five top winners. Can you figure out what place ribbon each of the following campers received? Write their names on the ribbons. **Nick placed after Maria and before Isaac. Ann placed after Isaac and before Carl.**

Name

CAMP FIELD DAY

Field Day was planned for the week following the Water Competition. Field Day is always one of the most fun days at camp! This year, it was full of fun and surprises. Help the sentences below make sense by filling in the correct adjective form (more, most, worse, worst, better, best). The first one is done for you.

> To compare adjectives:
>
> If an adjective has two or more syllables use **more** or **most** instead of **er** or **est**.
>
> **Good** and **bad** have special forms for comparison.
> > **One** person, place, or thing: **good** or **bad**
> > **Two**: better or worse
> > **Three** or more: **best** or **worst**

1. The ____**most**____ unusual event was the egg-on-a-spoon race.

2. During the race Justin was _____ careful than Manuel.

3. However, the _____ thing happened to Justin.

4. As Justin approached the finish line first, in the _____ position, the raw egg dropped from his spoon and splattered on his shoe.

5. The wheelbarrow race was the _____ awkward event of the day.

6. Billy and Isaac were the _____ nervous.

7. Consequently, they got the _____ start.

8. Ann and Maria were the _____ skillful in their ability to maneuver.

9. Passing an orange from neck to neck was the _____ difficult event.

10. Carl was _____ careful than most campers when he passed the orange.

11. However, because it was the _____ slippery, it dropped and became a juicy, gooey mess.

12. Lisa had the _____ time trying to pass that messy orange to Isaac.

Write four sentences in which you use more, most, worse, worst, better, or best.

1. _____

2. _____

3. _____

4. _____

Name _____

MEET BILLY B. GOOD

Have you met camper Billy B. Good? He is famous here at Camp Lookout.
He is just the kind of camper you do not want to have around. Find out
why by reading about Billy. Fill in the correct adverbs in the following
sentences. The first one is done for you.

> When using adverbs to **compare two actions**, add **er** to
>   most short adverbs.
>
> To **compare three actions**, add **est** to most short adverbs.
>
> If an adverb has two or more syllables, add **more** or **most**.

1. Billy B. Good is the son of camp counselor, Mr. O. B. Good. Almost everyone thinks the
   father should handle his son ___*more firmly*___. (firmly)

2. Billy is known to many as the camp prankster. He awakens the _____ each
   morning. (early)

3. When he awakens, he sneaks around the mess hall _____ than anyone can
   imagine. (cleverly)

4. He moves the _____ in the kitchen. (fast)

5. There he exchanges sugar for salt in all the shakers, _____ than a fox.
   (skillfully)

6. _____ than not he is the first one to arrive for breakfast. (often)

7. He waits _____ than the rest of the campers for everyone to arrive. (eagerly)

8. In the mess hall, his laugh fills the room. It can be heard _____ than all the
   other campers' voices put together. (loudly)

9. In the afternoon, when campers are busy with activities, Billy
   is working _____ than ever. (busily)

10. He sneaks in each cabin and works _____ than
    a mouse. (quietly)

11. He works _____ than most campers would ever
    consider. His work consists of putting frogs and ants in
    sleeping bags, exchanging items in campers' suitcases, and
    switching the boys' and girls' restroom signs. (long)

12. Even though he is treated _____ than other
    campers by the counselors, his pranks still continue. (harshly)

Name

GETTING NOWHERE

Ten adventuresome campers are going on a trail ride. Discover what happens on their ride!
As you read, choose the correct word to fill in the blank.

Words that mean **no** are called **negatives.**

Examples: not, never, nowhere, nothing, nobody, no one, aren't, doesn't, haven't, wouldn't.

Two negatives **should not be used** in the same sentence.

1. Not one of them _____ have missed going on the trail ride, except maybe Manuel. (would, wouldn't)

2. Manuel hadn't _____ been on a horse before. (never, ever)

3. He was assigned Pokey. Nobody else would have _____ to do with that horse on a trail ride. (nothing, anything)

4. Manuel could hear the other riders' voices far away in the distance. "Doesn't _____ want to ride with me?" he complained. (nobody, anybody)

5. Pokey smelled the flowers and chewed grass. There wasn't _____ he didn't enjoy seeing or eating. (nothing, anything)

6. It was for sure that Manuel and Pokey were getting _____ fast. (nowhere, anywhere)

7. The other riders had brought lunches, but hungry Manuel had not brought _____ . (anything, nothing)

8. He had hoped to get a horse fast enough to bring him back by lunchtime, but Pokey would have _____ to do with his schedule. (anything, nothing)

9. Suddenly, in the middle of the trail, Pokey stopped and wouldn't move for what seemed like hours. Manuel could get _____ to help. They were all too far ahead. (no one, anyone)

10. He tried pushing and pulling him, but there wasn't _____ he could do to make him move. (anything, nothing)

11. Manuel and Pokey had barely ridden beyond the stables. In the distance, they could hear voices. "We haven't gone _____ !" said Manuel bitterly. (nowhere, anywhere)

12. "Where have you been?" asked the riders. It wasn't _____ Manuel wanted to talk about. (anything, nothing)

Name

PICTURING PREPOSITIONS

Find out what is happening today at Camp Lookout. Begin practicing by underlining the prepositions in the sentences below. Check the first example.

> A **preposition** is a word that shows a relationship with other words in a sentence.
>
> A **prepositional phrase** includes the preposition, the object, and all the words in between.
>
> *Example: The bugs were crawling inside the sandwiches.*
> *In this sentence, **inside** is the preposition,*
> *and **inside the sandwiches** is the prepositional phrase.*

1. Ann was reading her book <u>in</u> the tree house.
2. The chipmunk was running across the boat dock.
3. Both Justin and Isaac could be found inside the mess hall.
4. She was afraid an alien was under her bed.
5. He was hiding between the pool and the cabins.
6. The horses were walking down the steep trail.

Next, use the prepositions below and the picture clues on the next page to make prepositional phrases. Write phrases that actually tell about something going on in the picture on page 35! Use these prepositions:

along   through   inside   from   between   behind

across   in   outside   under   around   beside   down   up   below

1. The snake was **<u>under the bed.</u>**
2. The bear was pawing _____.
3. The frog was _____.
4. Lisa climbed _____.
5. Manuel paddled his kayak _____.
6. Campers were singing _____.
7. Bigfoot was standing _____.
8. Maria caught an enormous fish _____.
9. Isaac was found _____.
10. The sailboat sailed _____.

Write five more sentences with prepositional phrases about the picture. Use another piece of paper. Use with page 35.

Name _____

CABIN 1

CAMP LOOKOUT!

Use with page 34.

GO FISH

It's time to do some fishing. Circle the direct object in each sentence. Then fish around in the word search pond. If the object you have circled is correct, you will be able to find it in the pond. There is only one direct object in each sentence. Good luck!

> The **direct object** is a noun or pronoun that receives the action of the verb.
>
> *Example: The squirrel ate acorns in the tree.*
> *Squirrel, a noun, is the subject. Ate is the verb. Acorns is a noun and the direct object.*

1. Manuel and Justin dug worms.
2. Maria packed several lunches for the trip.
3. Heidi searched the cabins for fishing gear.
4. The campers searched the creek for their favorite fishing spot.
5. They noticed deer nearby.
6. They located a good fishing hole.
7. Manuel cast his line into the water.
8. The line caught Justin's cap on the way.
9. Justin's cap splashed the water as it hit.
10. Heidi climbed a rock and knelt over the water trying to retrieve the cap.
11. Maria pulled a huge fish out of the water after her first cast.
12. Maria fed her friends the fish for dinner.

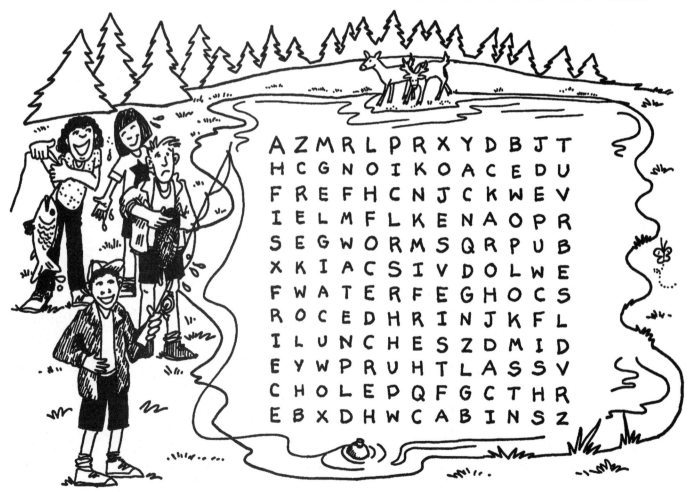

```
A Z M R L P R X Y D B J T
H C G N O I K O A C E D U
F R E F H C N J C K W E V
I E L M F L K E N A O P R
S E G W O R M S Q R P U B
X K I A C S I V D O L W E
F W A T E R F E G H O C S
R O C E D H R I N J K F L
I L U N C H E S Z D M I D
E Y W P R U H T L A S S V
C H O L E P Q F G C T H R
E B X D H W C A B I N S Z
```

Name _____

TAKEN BY STORM

Swimming in the Camp Lookout pool is one of the most popular activities. Below is a description of a day in the pool. Fill in the blanks with one of the homophones listed below so the description will make sense.

> **Homophones** are words that sound the same but are spelled differently.

they're   there   their   to   two   too   for   four

your   you're   by   bye   buy

1. Many campers were walking from _____ cabins _____ the swimming pool.

2. Some ran, hoping _____ be the first ones _____ .

3. Campers jumped in the water _____ and _____ at a time.

4. They left _____ towels _____ the grassy area.

5. "_____ running _____ fast along the edge of the pool!" yelled a counselor _____ the lifeguard.

6. The lifeguard, Ima Float, was _____ busy _____ notice what the children were doing.

7. "_____ being a nuisance," Ima called. "Mind _____ own business," she said as she continued putting on makeup and combing her hair.

8. Campers could _____ refreshments at a stand _____ the pool entrance.

9. _____ was lots of time for campers to eat and do _____ swimming tricks.

10. Maria and Heidi began doing _____ tricks in the water.

11. They did a handstand and _____ somersaults.

12. _____ hoping to get into water ballet classes some day.

13. Billy did a cannonball near _____ heads.

14. "Watch out, you big, bully billy goat!" yelled Maria. "_____ jumping too close to us."

15. All of a sudden, _____ was lightning and thunder. It began _____ pour.

16. "Grab _____ towels and run," yelled Ima, as the makeup dripped down her face.

17. Campers grabbed _____ towels, dressed quickly, and headed _____ _____ cabins. Snug and safe inside, they listened _____ the storm and played games.

Name _____

GETTING THE PICTURE

Isaac has made a drawing of Camp Lookout. Look on the next page (page 39) to see it. Notice that he made quite a few spelling mistakes when he labeled it. Cross out the errors and write the correct words. Five of them are already labeled correctly. After you finish, choose fifteen sets of the homophones below and write a sentence that uses all the words in the set. See the first example.

> **Homophones** are words that sound the same but are spelled differently.

tow toe   **sent cent scent**   **braid brayed**   **pair pare pear**

for four   **bare bear**   **night knight**   **dear deer**

hair hare   **flea flee**   **sale sail**   **whole hole**   **eye I**

meat meet   **pale pail**   **peace piece**   **bee be**   **wood would**

plane plain   **flour flower**   **horse hoarse**   **son sun**

*The bear is at **peace** while eating the **piece** of meat.*

1. _____
2. _____
3. _____
4. _____
5. _____
6. _____
7. _____
8. _____
9. _____
10. _____
11. _____
12. _____
13. _____
14. _____
15. _____

Use with page 39.

Name

Use with page 38.

RAPIDLY FALLING

Manuel is headed for the waterfall! Keep him from going over it by finding the contractions in these sentences. Circle all eleven, and write the words that form each contraction.

YOU'D BETTER WATCH OUT!

Oh, Oh!

> A **contraction** is a shortened word formed by combining two words. An **apostrophe** takes the place of any letters that are left out.
> *(could + not = couldn't)*

1. It wasn't sunny, but it was hot when Manuel went rafting down the Blue River. _____

2. "I'll be fine by myself," he told the counselor when he left. _____

3. He loves to raft, but he hasn't had much experience. _____

4. When rafting, it's important to know how to paddle properly through the rapids. _____

5. There weren't as many rapids as Manuel had expected. _____

6. Because the river seemed so calm, Manuel spent lots of time watching the wild life and didn't see what was looming up ahead. _____

7. It was unfortunate that he wasn't paying more attention. _____

8. It wouldn't be long until he'd reach a waterfall. _____

9. He'd be in for a big surprise. _____

10. Close your eyes. Don't look! _____

Write four sentences with contractions, and write the two words that make each contraction.

1. _____

2. _____

3. _____

4. _____

Name _____

STORM HITS CAMP LOOKOUT

The following news article was handed to the editor of a local newspaper. There are 31 errors in capitalization. Can you find them? Circle every letter that should be capitalized.

VOL. 26 ISSUE 38 JULY 5, 1998
75¢

storm hits camp lookout

there were more than the usual fireworks on tuesday evening, the fourth of july. around midnight a big storm hit camp lookout. luckily most of the campers were asleep in their cabins. hailstones the size of golf balls pelted the wooden structures. one of the campers, maria, was quoted as saying, "the ground shook with each clap of thunder, and the sky was fully lit every few minutes. we thought it would never end."

several campers did not have the protection of a cabin. nick, isaac, and manuel had decided to spend the night camping in a tent in the nearby hills. the tent collapsed on them during the storm. a rescue crew was called, including dr. smith, who is a part of the camp lookout staff. when the crew arrived, isaac said, "i was wondering about something—what took you so long?" the boys were found in safe, wet, exhausted condition.

INSIDE ☆
INTERVIEW WITH
IMA FLOAT ✱ ✱ ✱
LIFEGUARD AT
CAMP LOOKOUT.
☆ PAGE 8

BIG 🌲 WOODS PUBLISHING

SUBSCRIPTION IS
$39.00 PER YEAR.

☐ YOUR
SUBSCRIPTION
EXPIRES THE
MONTH SHOWN
ON YOUR ADDRESS
LABEL.

Name

UNBELIEVABLE NEWS

The following news article needs to be checked for proper capitalization before it is sent to the local newspaper editor. Make corrections, and rewrite the article on the lines below.

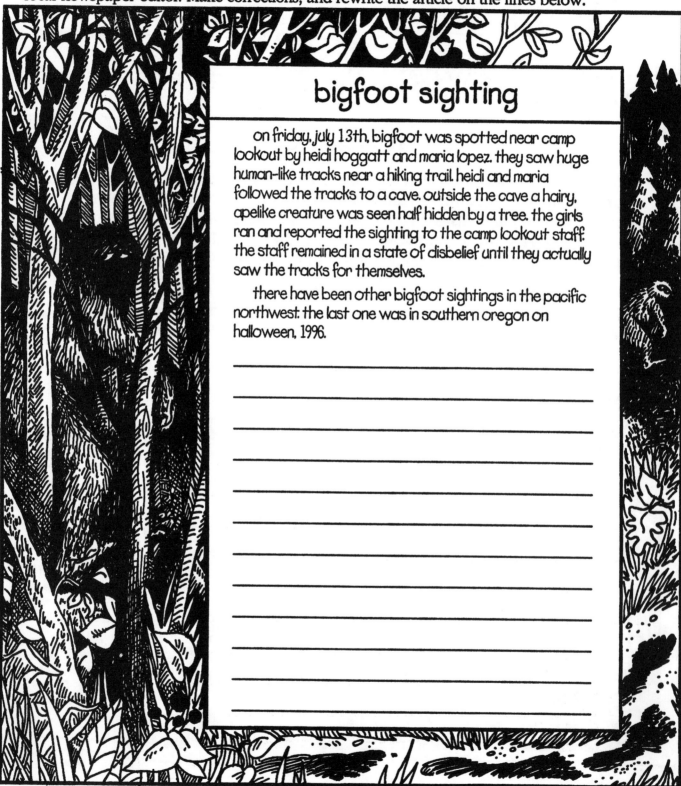

bigfoot sighting

on friday, july 13th, bigfoot was spotted near camp lookout by heidi hoggatt and maria lopez. they saw huge human-like tracks near a hiking trail. heidi and maria followed the tracks to a cave. outside the cave a hairy, apelike creature was seen half hidden by a tree. the girls ran and reported the sighting to the camp lookout staff. the staff remained in a state of disbelief until they actually saw the tracks for themselves.

there have been other bigfoot sightings in the pacific northwest. the last one was in southern oregon on halloween, 1996.

Name

42

A TRULY FREAKY STORM!

The following news article needs to be checked for proper capitalization before it is sent to the newspaper editor. Make corrections and rewrite the article on the lines below.

tornado hits

a freak storm hit the camp lookout area on wednesday, june 3. tornadoes are rarely seen in this part of the united states. luckily, there were no injuries. however, there were two unusual incidents. an outhouse was lifted by the tornado and moved to another location in the campground. fortunately, no one was in it at the time. the tornado also lifted all the frogs from a nearby pond and dropped them on some campers near the horse riding stables. justin loftus was quoted as saying, "from now on, let's say it's raining cats and *frogs*."

Name

A CAMPER'S MIDNIGHT HIKE

Isaac wrote a journal entry about his experience on a midnight hike. He forgot to include punctuation. See if you can add all the missing marks.

July 24 1997

Dear Diary

Last night we went on a great adventure Our cabin took a midnight hike with our cabin counselor Mr O B Good He is from Boise Idaho I think he's impatient and quite old He's lucky to have us kids in his cabin Were really a good fun bunch It took a while for us to get out of camp Before we started up a mountain trail we heard Carl squeal We all got freaked out thinking maybe it was Bigfoot or something but it was only Nick He had brought a water balloon and hit Carl in the back We all thought it was funny Our counselor asked When are you going to grow up I thought this was an odd question It seems a little early to be worrying about that

The trails were hard to see so we had fun using our flashlights We'd shine them in each others faces and have laser battles They also helped us to spot deer raccoons coyotes possums and a skunk When Manuel saw the skunk he yelled Yikes We're going to get sprayed We all ran as fast as we could Justin didn't run fast enough so he had to take a bath in tomato juice

Yours truly
Isaac

Use with page 45.

Name

A COUNSELOR'S MIDNIGHT HIKE

The camp counselor, Mr. O. B. Good, wrote a journal entry about his experience on a midnight hike. He forgot to include punctuation. See if you can add all the missing marks.

July 24 1997

CAMP LOOKOUT

Dear Diary

Last night I took the boys in our cabin on a midnight hike It was a disaster I'm young (forty) and think of myself as having a lot of patience but last night tested my limits These boys behave worse than any kids in the whole camp They're always arguing never minding me and playing jokes on each other Nick had the nerve to bring a water balloon on the hike He hit Carl in the back I almost returned them to our cabin I should have

I asked the kids to stay on the trails and they claimed they couldn't see them This was not true since there was a full moon and they had flashlights They used their flashlights as weapons to zap each other This was a constant thorn in my side However the worst experience of the hike was when we saw a skunk Manuel warned everyone by yelling We're going to get sprayed Complete chaos broke loose for everyone except Justin He has to be the slowest moving snail on the planet so of course he got sprayed The smell was horrible The kids went wild It was all I could do to get us safely back to camp

After getting the kids to their bunks I had the job of filling a tub with tomato juice I brought Justin to the tub and told him to get in He acted like I'd lost my mind And I had

Painfully yours

O B

Use with page 44.

Name

HELLO MOTHER, HELLO FATHER

Some of the campers are writing home. Their postcards, on this page and the next, need some punctuation and capitalization so the parents will be able to read them.
Edit each one, and rewrite it on the
lines below.

hello mother hello father
    here i am at camp lookout camp is very entertaining i went rafting and almost went down a waterfall i went fishing and caught justins hat i went horseback riding on the slowest horse in the world. pokey i had frog legs for dinner and oh yes i saw an alien can i stay longer
    xoxoxo, manuel

_____

_____

_____

_____

_____

_____

dear mom and dad
camp is fun i got lost for a day and a tornado hit our camp the counselor asks me to do fun stuff like take an owl raccoon and bag of marshmallows across the lake in a kayak the food is great

your loving son carl

_____

_____

_____

_____

_____

_____

Use with page 47.

Name

Edit and rewrite the postcards on this page also.

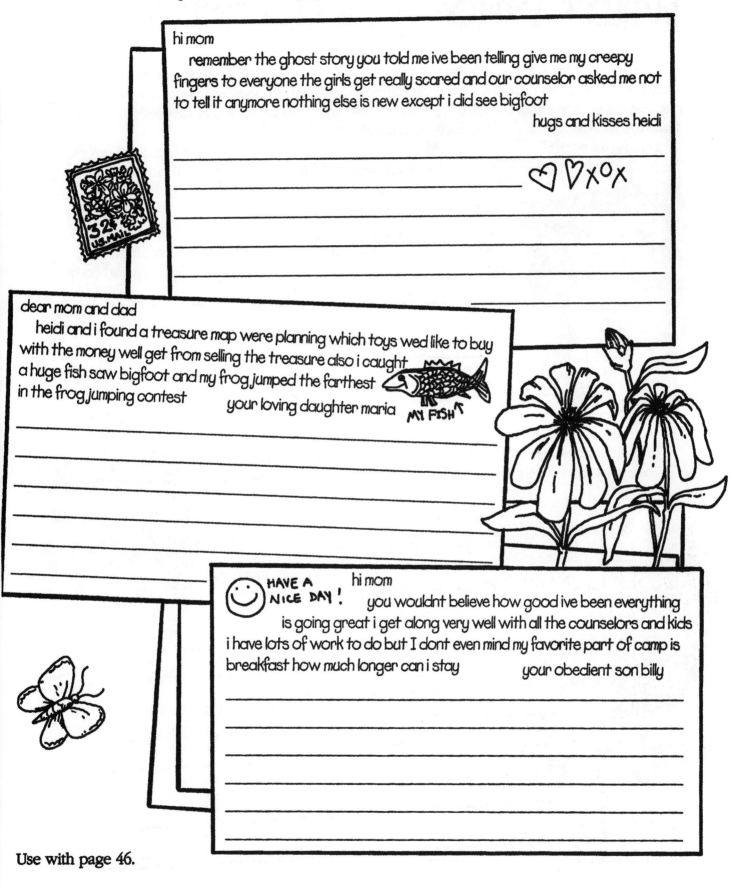

hi mom

remember the ghost story you told me ive been telling give me my creepy fingers to everyone the girls get really scared and our counselor asked me not to tell it anymore nothing else is new except i did see bigfoot

hugs and kisses heidi

dear mom and dad

heidi and i found a treasure map were planning which toys wed like to buy with the money well get from selling the treasure also i caught a huge fish saw bigfoot and my frog jumped the farthest in the frog jumping contest

your loving daughter maria

MY FISH

HAVE A NICE DAY!

hi mom

you wouldnt believe how good ive been everything is going great i get along very well with all the counselors and kids i have lots of work to do but I dont even mind my favorite part of camp is breakfast how much longer can i stay

your obedient son billy

Use with page 46.

Name

WHO'S WHO?

The Camp Lookout staff has a bunch of interesting characters! Here are some descriptions written by one of the campers for the camp newsletter. You can help get this article ready for publication by correcting the spelling errors before it goes to press. Circle misspelled words. Write the words correctly below each description.

The Cook, 12 errors   Arts and Crafts Coordinator, 11 errors   Lifeguard, 15 errors

Head Counselor, 14 errors   Campfire Song Leader, 13 errors   Trail Horse, 15 errors

THE COOK — Sir Loin

Sir Loin is originally frum England. He gratuated frum a gourmet cookin skool in Podunk, Kansas. His laghter is allways herd as he is surving the campers there food. His faverit food is Spam and crakers.

_____   _____   _____

_____   _____   _____

_____   _____   _____

_____   _____   _____

HEAD COUNSELOR — Mr. I. M. Wacky

Mr. Wacky is nown for making strainge reqests lik asking Carl to tak an owl, a racoon, and a bag of marshmellows accross the lake. At mealtime he is allways going bak for secunds. His faverit thing to do is clime the camp flagpoll.

_____   _____   _____

_____   _____   _____

_____   _____   _____

_____   _____

_____   _____

ARTS AND CRAFTS COORDINATOR —
Ms. Bea Creative

Ms. Creative clames, that unfonunately, she is allergic to glew. She injoys giving paterns to campers to trace and coler for there art activity. She doesnt lik to get dirty. Her faverit thing to do is clean hous.

_____   _____   _____

_____   _____   _____

_____   _____   _____

_____   _____

Use with page 49.

Name

WHO'S WHO? cont.

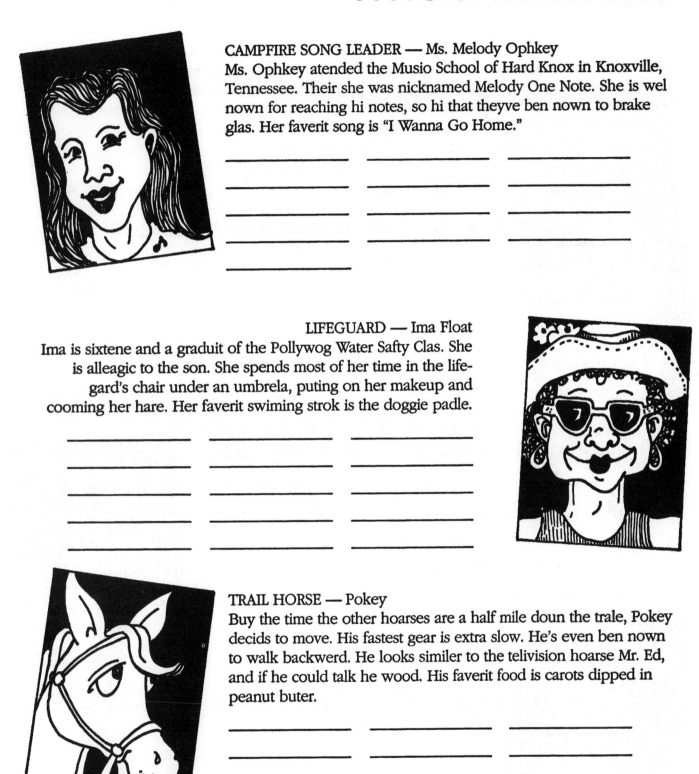

CAMPFIRE SONG LEADER — Ms. Melody Ophkey
Ms. Ophkey atended the Musio School of Hard Knox in Knoxville, Tennessee. Their she was nicknamed Melody One Note. She is wel nown for reaching hi notes, so hi that theyve ben nown to brake glas. Her faverit song is "I Wanna Go Home."

_____ _____ _____

_____ _____ _____

_____ _____ _____

_____ _____ _____

_____

LIFEGUARD — Ima Float
Ima is sixtene and a graduit of the Pollywog Water Safty Clas. She is alleagic to the son. She spends most of her time in the life-gard's chair under an umbrela, puting on her makeup and cooming her hare. Her faverit swiming strok is the doggie padle.

_____ _____ _____

_____ _____ _____

_____ _____ _____

TRAIL HORSE — Pokey
Buy the time the other hoarses are a half mile doun the trale, Pokey decids to move. His fastest gear is extra slow. He's even ben nown to walk backwerd. He looks similer to the telivision hoarse Mr. Ed, and if he could talk he wood. His faverit food is carots dipped in peanut buter.

_____ _____ _____

_____ _____ _____

_____ _____ _____

_____ _____ _____

Use with page 48.

Name _____

TREASURE HUNT

The map below was found by Heidi and Maria. They hope to discover buried treasure somewhere close to Camp Lookout. Unfortunately, there are many errors in the directions, and the map is hard for them to read. Help by rewriting the directions with correct punctuation, capitalization, and spelling. You will need to use a separate piece of paper for this task. Then follow the directions, and put an **X** on the spot where you think the treasure is hidden.

bigin at the boat dock SALE NORTHEAST ACCROSS AGATE LAKE
to the ALIEN Sighting WALK ALONG BEAR Creek UNTILL YOU
GIT TO BLUE riVER WALK tHREW the bear habitat WACH out
FER BARES TAKE A raFT WeST ON BLUE riVER
UNTILL YoU Git too the CaMPFiRe TAK A SWIM IN tHe PooL
AND WHeN YouR DUN USE THe BATHRUMS iF NeSiSARY
Go PASSeD the CABiNS AN the out hous to the BiGFoot
SightiNGS NoW WalK eAST the tReSUR iS BARiED UNDeR
A PiLe oF RoKS UNSCRAMBLe THiS sekRit CoDe TWO
FiGUR oUT WHeRe YoU DiG

yb___ the___ ohsre_____ gdirin____ bslstae_____

Use with page 50.

Name

CAMPSIDE CAPERS

Somebody's having a great old time in the camp garbage tonight. One camper has been sneaking around quietly to listen in on their conversation. This camper has written down everything Freddy Raccoon and Moe Mouse have said, but something is missing!

Insert quotation marks before and after the exact words that are being said. Write the conversations into the talk balloons for the animals. These words in the balloons will not need any quotation marks or explanations about who is talking!

Raiders of the Camp Cans

Tonight we'll raid the garbage cans outside the mess hall. Are you ready? asked Freddy.

You bet! exclaimed Moe.

There's a gold mine in this can! There's even a book. Have you ever read *Monster Madness?* asked Moe.

No! Why are you messing with books? I hear a noise. Grab your stuff and run, said Freddy.

I got corn cobs, potato peels, apple cores, bread crusts, and some mozzarella cheese. Yummm. What did you get? questioned Freddy.

Moe answered cheerfully, It looks like I got everything but the kitchen sink.

Name

52

APPENDIX

CONTENTS

GRAMMAR & USAGE GUIDE

SENTENCES AND SENTENCE PARTS

A **sentence** is made up of one or more words that express a complete thought.

A **declarative sentence** makes a statement. It tells something about a person, place, thing, or idea and ends with a period.

An **interrogative sentence** asks a question and ends with a question mark.

An **imperative sentence** makes a command and ends with a period.

An **exclamatory sentence** communicates strong emotion or surprise and ends with an exclamation point.

A **simple sentence** has only one complete thought.

A **compound sentence** is made of one or more simple sentences joined.

A **sentence fragment** is an incomplete sentence.

A **run-on sentence** contains two or more sentences that should be broken apart.

The **subject** of a sentence is the sentence part that names the thing or person doing something.

The **simple subject** is the subject without any words to describe it.

The **predicate** of a sentence tells what the person or thing is doing.

The **simple predicate** is the verb without the words to describe it.

PARTS OF SPEECH—NOUNS & PRONOUNS

A **noun** is a word that names a person, place, thing, or idea.

A **common noun** does not name a specific person, place, thing, or idea.

A **proper noun** names a specific person, place, thing, or idea.

A **plural noun** names more than one person, place, thing, or idea.

A **possessive noun** is a noun that shows ownership.

A **pronoun** is a word used in place of a noun.

A **subject pronoun** is used as the subject of the sentence.

An **object pronoun** is used in place of a noun and follows an action verb.

A **direct object** is a noun that receives the action directly from the verb.

PARTS OF SPEECH—VERBS

A **verb** expresses action or being.

A **present tense verb** expresses action that is happening now or continually.

A **past tense verb** expresses action that happened in the past.

A **future tense verb** expresses action that will happen in the future.

A **helping verb** helps to form some of the tenses of the main verb.

PARTS OF SPEECH—ADJECTIVES & ADVERBS

An **adjective** is a word used to describe a noun or pronoun. (Adjectives usually tell *which, what kind,* or *how many.*)

A **comparative adjective** compares two persons, places, things, or ideas.

A **superlative adjective** compares three or more persons, places, things, or ideas.

An **adverb** describes a verb, adjective, or another adverb. (Adverbs tell *when, where, how often, how long,* or *how.*)

PARTS OF SPEECH—PREPOSITIONS

A **preposition** is a word that shows how two words are related. (*Examples: under, in, around.*)

A **prepositional phrase** is a group of words that begins with a preposition and includes the object of the preposition and other words. (*Into the tent* is a prepositional phrase.)

CAPITALIZE:

- the first word in every sentence
- the first word in a direct quotation
- all proper nouns and adjectives
- the first word in the greeting and closing of a letter
- names of people, places, days, months, countries, languages, races, nationalities, holidays, documents, historical events, organizations, and businesses
- the first letter of all words in a title except articles and prepositions

PUNCTUATION

- End declarative and imperative sentences with a period.
- Follow initials and abbreviations with a period.
- Separate items in a list with commas.
- Use commas to separate words in dates and addresses.
- End questions with a question mark.
- End exclamations with an exclamation point.
- Use an apostrophe to form the possessive of a noun.
- Use an apostrophe to show where letters are missing in a contraction.
- Put quotation marks around the words being said in a direct quotation.
- Underline or italicize titles of magazines, books, movies, and plays.

GRAMMAR & USAGE
SKILLS TEST

Questions 1 through 95 are worth 1 point each. Question 96 is worth 5 points.

Identify the following sentences by writing . . .
  D for **declarative sentence**   **EX** for **exclamatory sentence**
  IM for **imperative sentence**   **I** for **interrogative sentence**

_____ 1. How do we get to Camp Lookout?

_____ 2. Watch out for scorpions!

_____ 3. Did you put the frogs in the boys' bunks?

_____ 4. Please don't feed the bears.

_____ 5. It's time to put up the tent.

Identify the following sentences by writing . . .
  S for **simple sentence**   **R** for **run-on sentence**
  C for **compound sentence**   **F** for **sentence fragment**

_____ 6. Going over the waterfall.

_____ 7. Eat your breakfast, and clean your cabins.

_____ 8. Turn left at the stump take three steps north enter the cave.

_____ 9. What a cute squirrel in your tent!

_____ 10. Did you step in the poison ivy?

Write the simple subject for each sentence on the line.

_____ 11. Sam raced us to the diving board.

_____ 12. Were the bears eating your marshmallows?

_____ 13. The biggest chipmunk took my backpack.

Write the simple predicate for each sentence on the line.

_____ 14. Falling rocks crashed into the campsite.

_____ 15. Could crafty coyotes catch cunning campers?

_____ 16. We watched while the wind blew our tent away.

Identify the parts of speech in the sentence below by writing . . .
  N for **noun**   **V** for **verb**
  ADJ for **adjective**   **ADV** for **adverb**
  Three hungry campers gobbled pancakes greedily.

_____ 17. Three   _____ 20. gobbled

_____ 18. hungry   _____ 21. pancakes

_____ 19. campers   _____ 22. greedily

Name

Read the following sentence, and look for the nouns. Decide if the nouns are common or proper.

Last Friday, Billy put spiders in the beds and hot pepper in the soup.

_____ 23. Write the common nouns from the sentence.

_____ 24. Write the proper nouns from the sentence.

Write the plural form of each word below.

_____ 25. compass

_____ 26. knife

_____ 27. tomato

_____ 28. deer

_____ 29. family

Write the singular form of each word below.

_____ 30. mice

_____ 31. children

_____ 32. cities

Write a possessive noun phrase (two words) to fit each description.

_____ 33. teeth belonging to one fox

_____ 34. teeth belonging to more than one fox

_____ 35. shirts belonging to three campers

_____ 36. tail of one skunk

Write the subject pronoun from each sentence.

_____ 37. They couldn't decide where to pitch their tent.

_____ 38. She said that the task was too hard.

Write the object pronoun from each sentence.

_____ 39. Don't ask him for help.

_____ 40. We gave them a ride on the donkey.

Write the correct form (tense) of the verb needed in the sentence. Find the verb at the end of each sentence.

_____ 41. Yesterday, Carl _____ boats for a contest. (row)

_____ 42. This morning, Lisa _____ away from the sinking boat. (swim)

_____ 43. Oh, no! Matt _____ off his raft into the river! (fall)

_____ 44. Tomorrow our cabin _____ kites. (fly)

_____ 45. Who _____ my green pajamas last night? (wear)

_____ 46. How many campers _____ to their parents this week? (write)

_____ 47. She _____ when she saw the lizard in her shoe. (faint)

_____ 48. Last night we _____ to replace the cook. (vote)

Name _____

Write the action verb from each sentence.

_____ 49. Lisa screamed at the top of her lungs!

_____ 50. She was there when Maria jumped out of the closet.

_____ 51. Lisa crept underneath the covers.

Write the helping verb from each sentence.

_____ 52. He is playing with matches.

_____ 53. Tom should start getting wood for the campfire.

_____ 54. Bigfoot is coming!

_____ 55. Is it true that you have seen a spaceship?

Identify each part of speech shown at the end of the sentence by writing . . .
    N for **noun**   **V** for **verb**   **ADJ** for **adjective** **ADV** for **adverb**

_____ 56. Eat your grilled cheese sandwich. (Eat)

_____ 57. Watch the song leader closely. (closely)

_____ 58. Don't you just love the beautiful camp theme song? (beautiful)

_____ 59. Who won the frog jumping contest? (contest)

_____ 60. Counselor Wacky fell out of the canoe. (fell)

_____ 61. That meat loaf was the most terrible food yet! (terrible)

_____ 62. Back away slowly from the rattlesnake. (slowly)

Write the correct form of the adjective that should be placed in the blank. The adjectives are shown at the end of the sentence.

_____ 63. Karl's race was _____ than Isaac's. (fast)

_____ 64. Whose frog jumped the _____ ? (farther)

_____ 65. This is the _____ lunch meat I've ever seen! (slimy)

Write the adjective form that will correctly fill in the blank.

_____ 66. This is the _____ pizza I have ever eaten. (better, best)

_____ 67. I have eaten a lot, but it is still ____ than you've eaten. (less, least)

_____ 68. My score was the _____ of all the runners. (worse, worst)

Write the adverb form that will correctly fill in the blank.

_____ 69. Billy gets up _____ than the other campers. (early)

_____ 70. He plays pranks _____ than the other campers. (often)

_____ 71. Nick can climb the flagpole the _____ of all of the campers. (quickly)

Choose the word that will show the correct use of a negative.

_____ 72. No one (would, wouldn't) want to miss the shooting stars.

_____ 73. The campers have not gotten (any, no) mail today.

_____ 74. Won't (anyone, no one) come to the haunted cabin with me?

_____ 75. We don't (never, ever) want to go there again.

Name

Write the preposition from each sentence.

_____ 76. Just what do you have hidden under your bed?

_____ 77. Let's push the counselors into the pool.

_____ 78. I will race you across the campground.

Write the prepositional phrase from each sentence.

_____ 79. Bigfoot is standing behind you.

_____ 80. Please walk around the flowers.

_____ 81. There's some rotten food beneath your bed.

Write the direct object from each sentence.

_____ 82. Let's go down to the river and dig some worms.

_____ 83. Grab your towels and run!

_____ 84. After dinner, we'll play some good pranks on the boys.

Write the two words used to form each contraction.

_____ 85. won't   _____ 87. I've

_____ 86. they're   _____ 88. we'd

Write the correct homophone in each blank.

_____ 89. I've gotten a little (horse, hoarse) from yelling so much.

_____ 90. Watch out! Don't step in that (hole, whole)!

_____ 91. Let's (meet, meat) behind the horse stables at midnight.

_____ 92. That just doesn't make any (cents, sense).

Find the misspelled words in the sentences, and write them correctly on the line.

The cook at are camp allways creats the most delichus meels.
We have our faverite pizza wunce a weak and marshmellows every day for desert!

93. _____

_____

Circle the words that should have capital letters in each sentence.

94. camp begins on sunday and ends on friday each week in july.

95. counselor joe told lisa to write to her parents.

Add the missing punctuation to the letter below.

96.

Dear Mom and Dad   July 15 1997
I am having the best time at this camp You won't believe how well Im doing
We have terrible food lots of mosquitoes and grumpy counselors Doesn't it
sound great I think I saw an alien and I fell out of the canoe three times
How much longer can I stay

Your loving son
Manuel

Total Score _____ out of 100 points.

Name _____

ANSWER KEY

SKILLS TEST

1. I
2. EX
3. I
4. IM
5. D
6. F
7. C
8. R
9. F
10. S
11. Sam
12. bears
13. chipmunk
14. crashed
15. could catch
16. watched, blew
17. ADJ
18. ADJ
19. N
20. V
21. N
22. ADV
23. spiders, beds, pepper, soup
24. Friday, Billy
25. compasses
26. knives
27. tomatoes
28. deer
29. families
30. mouse
31. child
32. city
33. fox's teeth
34. foxes' teeth
35. campers' shirts
36. skunk's tail
37. They
38. She
39. him
40. them
41. rowed
42. swam
43. fell or is falling
44. will fly
45. wore
46. wrote or will write or are writing
47. fainted
48. voted
49. screamed
50. jumped
51. crept
52. is
53. should
54. is
55. have

56. V
57. ADV
58. ADJ
59. N
60. V
61. ADJ
62. ADV
63. faster
64. farthest
65. slimiest
66. best
67. less
68. worst
69. earlier
70. more often
71. most quickly
72. would
73. any
74. anyone
75. ever
76. under
77. into
78. across
79. behind you
80. around the flowers
81. beneath your bed
82. worms
83. towels
84. pranks
85. will not
86. they are
87. I have
88. we would or we had or we should
89. hoarse
90. hole
91. meet
92. sense
93. our, always, creates, delicious, meals, favorite, once, week, marshmallows, dessert
94. Camp, Sunday, Friday, July
95. Counselor, Joe, Lisa
96.

> July 15, 1997
>
> Dear Mom and Dad,
>
> I am having the best time at this camp! You won't believe how well I'm doing. We have terrible food, lots of mosquitoes, and grumpy counselors. Doesn't it sound great? I think I saw an alien, and I fell out of the canoe three times. How much longer can I stay?
>
> Your loving son,
> Manuel

SKILLS EXERCISES

page 10

Answers may vary slightly, as a choice between exclamatory and imperative statements is sometimes subjective.

1. I (?)
2. IM (.)
3. D (.)
4. D (.)
5. IM (.) or E (!)
6. IM (.)
7. E (!)
8. I (?)
9. I (?)
10. E (.) or IM (!)
11. D (.)
12. E (!)
13. D (.)

Camp Lookout is in Washington.
Sentence examples will vary.

page 11

10. tree house; is reached
9. coyote; howls
8. owl; hoots
7. Squirrels; jump
6. rope; hangs
5. Birds; have built
4. Moss; is growing
3. some; are falling
2. tree house; looks
1. ladder; shakes

page 12

S, C, S, C, S, C
S, S, S, S, S
Carl needs to do this:
Take the chipmunk across the lake and leave it. Go back, pick up the owl, take it across the lake, and leave it. Then pick up the chipmunk and bring it back across. Leave the chipmunk and take the marshmallows across the lake. Go back alone to pick up the chipmunk and bring it across the lake.

page 13

Answers will vary when students expand fragments into sentences on numbers 2, 3, 4, 6, 8, and 9.

1. The boulders rolled slowly at first. They gathered speed soon after.
5. The boulders crushed plants. Animals scampered away quickly.
7. They gained speed. Over and over they rolled.
10. The boulders are approaching Camp Lookout. Will they stop in time?

page 14

1. ADJ—The; ADJ—wooden; N—boat; V—sailed; ADV—smoothly
2. ADJ—The; ADJ—north; N—wind; V—blew; ADV—hard
3. ADJ—A; ADJ—colorful; N—sail; V—flapped; ADV—gracefully
4. ADV—Often; ADJ—a; ADJ—brown; N—squirrel; V—chews; N—acorns; ADJ—the; ADJ—boat; N—dock
5. ADJ—The; N—deer; V—were walking; ADV—slowly; ADJ—the; N—shore
6. ADV—Sometimes; ADJ—a; ADJ—curious; N—raccoon; V—rides; N—one; ADJ—the; N—sailboats
7. ADJ—The; ADJ—goofy; N—camper; V—fell; ADV—awkwardly; ADJ—the; N—water
8. ADJ—Two; N—campers; V—swam; ADV—quickly; V—rescue; ADJ—their; N—friend

page 15

1. Proper—Lisa; Common—key, outhouse
2. Proper—Friday, Billy; Common—key, raccoon
3. Proper—Lisa; Common—trail, snake, path
4. Common—coyote
5. Common—chipmunk, stump, key
6. Common—owl, key
7. Common—bear, berries, patch
8. Common—rabbit
9. Proper—Blue River; Common—shore, beaver, tree
10. Proper—Lisa; Common—skunk, way
11. Proper—August; Common—tracks, ones
12. Common—tracks; door

page 16

1. marshes
2. cities
3. compasses
4. holidays
5. songs
6. foxes
7. bushes
8. poles
9. bunches
10. branches
11. marshmallows
12. campers; bags

page 17

1. sheep
2. mice
3. Echoes
4. children
5. potatoes
6. teeth
7. loaves; knives
8. trout
9. tomatoes
10. radios
11. feet
12. lives
13. moose

page 18

Answers may vary some. Allow anything that makes sense.
1. tent's poles
2. skunk's babies
3. camper's compass
4. tree house's door
5. rabbit's ears
6. counselor's T-shirt
7. Bigfoot's footprints
8. fox's teeth
Sentences will vary.

page 19

1. flowers' petals
2. children's treasure map
3. cooks' aprons
4. mice's food
5. campers' sleeping bags
6. deer's tails
7. boats' sails
8. counselors' caps

page 20

These sentences have subject pronouns:
2. It
4. They
6. She
8. She
9. I
12. You
Sentences for bottom:
3. They were packing for their trip.
5. She had forgotten to include a flashlight.
7. She had packed too much.
10. She couldn't decide where to put her fishing gear.
11. It would not fit in the trunk of Maria's father's car.

page 21

1. us
2. him
3. her
4. them
5. us
6. it
7. us
8. them
9. me
10. them, us
11. him
12. us
Sentences at bottom will vary.

page 22

1. shines
2. sail
3. row
4. fish
5. drink
6. splashes
7. watches
8. build
9. roast
10. falls
11. skips
12. swim
Stories at bottom will vary.

page 23

1. watched
2. sprayed
3. fished
4. chewed
5. hovered
6. shared
7. talked
8. suggested
9. proposed
10. moved
11. floated
12. enjoyed
Stories at bottom will vary.

page 24

1. will go
2. will study
3. will bring
4. will try
5. will take
6. will be
7. will find
8. will fly
9. will look
10. will eat
11. will care
12. will hope
Stories at bottom will vary.

page 25

1. thought
2. saw
3. hid
4. grew
5. came
6. wore
7. ate
8. went

9. ran
10. flew
11. told
12. wrote
Sentences at bottom will vary.

page 26

Action verbs are:
noticed, appeared, scratched, wiggled, were playing, heard, whisper, crawled, sat, tried, was coming, noticed, did seem, attached, listened, creaked, opened, moved, hid, got, give, hid, heard, Give
Sentences at bottom will vary.

page 27

1. is
2. were
3. will
4. is
5. has
6. had
7. has
8. am
9. should
10. will
11. should
12. are; will
Check to see that student drawing follows maze accurately.

page 28

1. The, slimy, gooey
2. The, crunchy, purple, a
3. old, moldy, the
4. the, clumsy, a, French, dandelion
5. The, muddy, thick, cold, Maria's
6. the, a, tiny, tasty, frog, his
7. the, strange, sticky
8. Hungry, the, weird, grilled, cheese
   BOTTOM: strange; slimy; moldy
   Menu ideas will vary.

page 29

1. Immediately
2. slowly
3. patiently
4. down; carefully
5. firmly
6. quickly
7. loudly, softly
8. closely
9. early
10. Now, cheerfully, clearly

page 30

1. tiniest
2. larger
3. biggest
4. wettest
5. latest

6. slimiest
7. smallest
8. farthest
9. fattest
10. highest
11. longest
12. faster
13. slowest
14. fastest
Bottom: 1st—Maria
      2nd—Nick
      3rd—Isaac
      4th—Ann
      5th—Carl

page 31

1. most
2. more
3. worst
4. best
5. most
6. most
7. worst
8. most
9. most
10. more
11. most
12. worst (or best)
Sentences at bottom will vary.

page 32

1. more firmly
2. earliest
3. more cleverly
4. fastest
5. more skillfully
6. More often
7. more eagerly
8. more loudly
9. more busily
10. more quietly
11. longer
12. more harshly

page 33

1. would
2. ever
3. anything
4. anybody
5. anything
6. nowhere
7. anything
8. nothing
9. no one
10. anything
11. anywhere
12. anything

pages 34–35

1. in
2. across
3. inside

4. under
5. between
6. down
Bottom half of page—answers will vary.

page 36

1. worms
2. lunches
3. cabins
4. creek
5. deer
6. hole
7. line
8. cap
9. water
10. rock
11. fish
12. friends
Check puzzles to see that students have circled all the above words.

page 37

1. their, to
2. to, there
3. two, four
4. their, by
5. You're, too, to
6. too, to
7. You're, your
8. buy, by
9. There, their
10. their (or two)
11. two (or four)
12. They're (or You're)
13. their
14. You're
15. there, to
16. your
17. their, for (or to), their, to

page 39

Look at student art to see that they have crossed out the following words and have replaced them as shown:
plain = plane
son = sun
pare = pair
sale = sail
meet = meat
bare = bear
whole = hole
dear = deer
hair = hare
pale = pail
I = eye
tow = toe
night = knight
be = bee
hoarse = horse
flour = flower
Original sentences will vary.

Name

page 40

1. wasn't = was not
2. I'll = I will
3. hasn't = has not
4. it's = it is
5. weren't = were not
6. didn't = did not
7. wasn't = was not
8. wouldn't = would not; he'd = he would
9. He'd = he would
10. Don't = do not

Sentences at bottom will vary.

page 41

Words to be capitalized:
Storm, Hits, Camp, Lookout, There, Tuesday, Fourth, July, Around, Camp, Lookout, Luckily, Hailstones, One, Maria, The, We, Several, Nick, Isaac, Manuel, The, A, Dr., Smith, Camp, Lookout, When, Isaac, I, The

page 42

Words to be capitalized:
Bigfoot, Sighting, On, Friday, July, Bigfoot, Camp, Lookout, Heidi, Hoggatt, Maria, Lopez, They, Heidi, Maria, Outside, The, Camp, Lookout, The, There, Bigfoot, Pacific, Northwest, The, Oregon, Halloween

page 43

Words to be capitalized:
Tornado, Hits, A, Camp, Lookout, Wednesday, June, Tornadoes, United, States, Luckily, However, An, Fortunately, The, Justin, Loftus, From

page 44

Check student papers for proper punctuation.

page 45

Check student papers for proper punctuation.

page 46

Check student papers for accurate editing.

page 47

Check student papers for accurate editing.

pages 48–49

Misspelled words spelled correctly.
COOK:
from, graduated, from, cooking, school, laughter, always, heard, serving, their, favorite, crackers
HEAD COUNSELOR:
known, strange, requests, like, take, raccoon, marshmallows, across, always, back, seconds, favorite, climb, flagpole
ARTS & CRAFTS COORDINATOR:
claims, unfortunately, glue, enjoys, patterns, color, their, doesn't, like, favorite, house
CAMPFIRE SONG LEADER:
attended, Music, There, well, known, high, high, they've, been, known, break, glass, favorite
LIFEGUARD:
sixteen, graduate, safety, class, allergic, sun, lifeguard's, umbrella, putting, combing, hair, favorite, swimming, stroke, paddle

TRAIL HORSE:
By, horses, down, trail, decides, been, known, backward, similar, television, horse, would, favorite, carrots, butter

pages 50–51

Check student papers to see that all errors are properly identified and fixed. Scrambled words are: by the horse riding stables.
Check student maps to see that trails are accurate. X should be next to the pile of rocks by riding stables.

page 52

"Tonight we'll raid the garbage cans outside the mess hall. Are you ready?" asked Freddy.

"You bet!" exclaimed Moe.

"There's a gold mine in this can! There's even a book. Have you ever read *Monster Madness?*" asked Moe.

"No! Why are you messing with books? I hear a noise. Grab your stuff and run," said Freddy.

"I got corn cobs, potato peels, apple cores, bread crusts, and some mozzarella cheese. Yummm. What did you get?" questioned Freddy.

Moe answered cheerfully, "It looks like I got everything but the kitchen sink."